# LENORMAND BASICS

## HOW TO READ LENORMAND CARDS FOR BEGINNERS

### GREGORY LEE WHITE

Mojo Studio & Conjure Co. Publishing
Nashville, TN

Lenormand Basics
How to Read Lenormand Cards for Beginners
by
Gregory Lee White

Copyright © 2021 Gregory Lee White
gregoryleewhite.com

Text:
Gregory Lee White

Cover Art:
Gregory Lee White. Based on the box art for Mlle. Lenormand Fortune Telling
Playing Cards, Wahrsage Karten, 1880

Proofreading:
Roy Hamilton, Gregory White, Virginia Tabor

Interior Illustrations:
a varied collection of antique Lenormand and cartomancy card decks. Main card
pages from the 1926 Carreras Fortune Telling cards

First Edition 2021

Published by
The Mojo Studio and Conjure Co. Publishing
211 Donelson Pike, Suite 111
Nashville, Tn 37214

Printed in the Unites States

ISBN: 978-1-7379306-0-0

# TABLE OF CONTENTS

What are Lenormand Cards? ........................................................1

Who Was Marie Lenormand? ......................................................2

The Cards ..................................................................................9

Card Meanings .....................................................................11- 46

The Playing Card Suits in Lenormand ..................................... 47

Short History of Playing Cards .................................................. 48

A Timeline of Playing Cards ...................................................... 50

The Gypsy Witch "Lenormand" ................................................ 51

Playing Card Associations in Lenormand ................................ 52

Tea Leaf Reading Symbols ......................................................... 55

How to Read the Cards .............................................................. 59

Three Card Spread ...................................................................... 60

Cross Spread ............................................................................... 62

Nine-Card Spread ....................................................................... 64

The Grand Tableau ..................................................................... 67

Lenormand Houses ..................................................................... 69

The Four Corners ....................................................................... 70

Near and Far ............................................................................... 70

A Library of Lenormand ............................................................ 71

Conclusion .................................................................................. 81

Bibliography ............................................................................... 82

## OTHER BOOKS BY GREGORY LEE WHITE

Clucked – The Tale of Pickin Chicken

Making Soap from Scratch: How to Make Handmade Soap – A Beginners Guide and Beyond

Essential Oils and Aromatherapy - How to Use Essential Oils for Beauty, Health, and Spirituality

Little House Search – A Puzzle Book and Tour of the Works of Laura Ingalls Wilder

The Use of Magical Oils in Hoodoo, Prayer, and Spellwork

Papa Gee's Hoodoo Herbal - The Magic of Herbs, Roots, and Minerals in the Hoodoo Tradition

The Stranger in the Cup – How to Read Your Luck and Fate in the Tea Leaves by Gregory Lee White and Catherine Yronwode

How to Use Amulets, Charms, and Talismans in the Hoodoo and Conjure Tradition
by Catherine Yronwode and Gregory Lee White

# INTRODUCTION

I began my love of Lenormand cards out of my frustration in trying to learn the Tarot. It seemed like I could not get the hang of remembering all the multi-layered meanings of all 78 cards and how they fit together. As a practitioner of American folk magic, it wasn't until I made friends and acquaintances among Hoodoo practitioners that I first heard about Lenormand cards – obviously popular in that community. After buying my first deck, I was amazed that I knew how to read them in just one week. Something about them spoke to me, and I connected with them quickly. Ironically, after learning Lenormand, the meanings of the Tarot finally fell into place for me after years of frustrating study. My love of them led me to create my own deck back in 2013, The Good Mojo Lenormand, now in its fourth edition.

I once witnessed a conversation where a woman showed her friend the Rider card in a Lenormand deck and tried to assign particular meanings to the house and the trees in the background. This is incorrect. The focus of the card is the man riding the horse – the Rider, and only the rider. Anything in the background or foreground - even the color of his horse, has no underlying or psychological meaning. It very simply signifies that something is about to "ride into your life" – that delays are over, and things are about to happen. I like to appreciate Lenormand cards for what they are and respect their history, their own special place in the world of divination. We can begin this journey of respect by not trying to turn them into Tarot cards. They are not. Now, if you choose to read them this way in your personal practice, so be it. However, nothing will irk a faithful Lenormand card reader more than if you start teaching classes on Lenormand and begin tossing in Tarot associations (I've seen it happen.) Once again, Lenormand is not Tarot – never will be.

# DEDICATION

This book is dedicated to all the card readers, psychics, astrologers, and mediums who read and teach classes in our store, aromaG's Botanica. You help people every day to find the answers they seek.

# ACKNOWLEDGEMENTS

None of my books would be possible without the support and love of my husband, Roy. He gives me the space I need to go on a writing frenzy until, months later, I emerge somewhat normal again where he is waiting for me.

Much gratitude to my good friend, Catherine Yronwode, who made me a better publisher. Her detailed research, a demand for excellence, and her love affair with typography has been a guiding light.

A special thanks to all my clients for whom I read Tarot and Lenormand. I hope my readings give you a sense of clarity, comfort, and grounding.

# WHAT ARE LENORMAND CARDS?

Lenormand cards, originally known as *Petit Le Normand,* have been around since the late 18th century. But they were not designed as a means of divination. Much like the Tarot, they began as a parlor game. The Lenormand cards were initially known as "The Game of Hope," a creation of Johann Kasper Hechtel, a German businessman and designer of parlor games who lived in Nuremberg. As a game, the players would lay out the 36 cards in six rows of six and roll dice to proceed along the cards. Traditionally, each player began by choosing their mark, something that signified them as a player (think 'car' or 'top-hat' in Monopoly). Some cards were considered positive signs of good fortune and luck - others bad luck or misfortune. Each spot you landed on might force you back a few spaces or advance you forward. For example, if the player landed on the snake card, they had to go back three spaces to ensure their safety from the serpent. If they happened to land on the key card, however, they would advance two spaces. Land on the book? Sorry, you must go back to the Garden card. The entire game was won by landing on the Anchor card, known as the "hope card."

As time went on, and people continued to weave stories around the images while playing the game, they noticed that the imagery reflected events, large and small, that were happening in their lives. Eventually, they used the cards as divination tools to showcase and tell more about these life events. This act of storytelling through the cards is similar to an earlier 1775 deck called *Hooper's Conversation Cards*, a game in which the cards were used to

1

create a story one card at a time. Each player would choose a card, study its picture, and add to the storyline.

The main way Lenormand differs from Tarot is that each card has a very straightforward meaning. They address the meat and bones of what is going on in your life, leaving the psychological aspects for the Tarot to figure out. Through their universal symbols, Lenormand represents our path in life and the hardships we sometimes have to endure. There are matters of money, betrayal, choosing the right path, deception, planning for the future, love, communication, commitment, and settling down – just to name a few.

Much of the symbology of Lenormand cards coincide with the symbols used in tasseomancy, the art of reading tea leaves and coffee grounds. Some of the oldest decks dating back to around 1799 are currently kept in the British Museum in London. While doing research in the British Museum, Tarot scholar Mary Greer found a book in the archives describing a deck of 32 cards based on coffee ground divinatory images - an obvious early model for the *Petit Le Normand*. The deck was published in England in 1796. What she discovered was that nearly all of the 32 cards in the deck were the exact same imagery found in Lenormand: Rider, Clover, Anchor, Lily, Garden, Fish, Coffin, etc. The exceptions were a Lion in place of the Bear, a second bush-like tree that is believed to have been replaced by the Key symbol, and an Insects card that was replaced by the Fox card.

The description from the British Museum reads as follows: "A sequence of 32 playing-cards bound (at the British Museum) as a small book, having on them emblematic designs of various character, and below moral apophthegms to which the designs have reference. Each piece has a number at the upper left-hand corner answering to certain explanatory and descriptive tables given in a book of directions which accompanies the cards. The title page of this book of 31 pages bears the following lettered inscription: "Les Amusements des Allemands, or The Diversions of the Court of Vienna, in which the Mystery of Fortune-Telling from the Grounds of the Coffee-Cup is unravelled, and Three pleasant Games, viz.: 1. Fortune-telling from the Grounds of the Coffee-Cup. 2. Fortune-telling by laying out the cards. 3. The new Imperial Game of numbers are invented", and "London: Printed for Champante and Whitrow, Jewry-Street, Aldgate, and may be had at every Booksellers and Toy Shop in the Kingdom, 1796."

## WHO WAS MARIE LENORMAND?

The famous fortune teller, Marie Anne Adelaide Lenormand, was born on May 27, 1772, in Alençon, in France's Normandy region. She was the firstborn child of Jean Louis Antoine Lenormand (a draper by trade) and his wife, Marie Anne Guilbert Lenormand. Later came a younger brother and sister. However, only five years later, Jean Louis died, leaving behind his family of four to fend for themselves. As was the custom of the time, his widow quickly remarried for the sake of her children but fell ill herself and died a short time later. When the Lenormand children's stepfather married again, he sent the sisters away to a Benedictine convent boarding school and their younger brother to live with distant relatives.

It was in the house of the Benedictines that Marie began to demonstrate psychic ability. She predicted the Mother Superior would soon lose her place and be asked to step down. Since such abilities were not considered 'of God,' she was punished and instructed to do penance. When the time came that the Superior was to leave, Marie predicted the name of her successor successfully, proving her clairvoyant abilities.

In 1786, when she was only 14, Marie obtained permission from her stepfather for her to move to Paris, where he had found her work as a seamstress. She left the convent with only the clothes on her back and six shillings in her pocket. But Marie was ambitious and intelligent. Her employers recognized these qualities in her and taught her math and bookkeeping; both would come in handy one day when she was running her own business.

Wanting to explore her supernatural abilities more, Marie furthered her studies in the esoteric. During her time at the convent, she had access to libraries and studied books on Roman and Greek divination techniques, horoscopes, dream interpretations, and the mystical teaching of the Kabbalah. She went on to read about the ancient philosophers Plato and Socrates, who also interpreted dreams. She learned the art of palm reading then, later, how to incorporate the use of cards into her divination practice.

Now that her clairvoyant skills were accomplished and refined, she took her knowledge of the supernatural and her head for business and opened shop as a fortune teller (known as a 'seeress' at the time) at No 5 Rue de

*Mademoiselle Lenormand's Arrest (1772 – 1843) Seb. Leroy delineat & Fr. Janet sculpsit, 1814*

Tournon there in Paris. The sign on her door read 'libraire' (French for 'bookseller'), although her clients knew precisely what her shop had to offer inside. Her waiting room did offer reading materials, giving it the appearance of a place to purchase literature. However, it was also adorned with unusual artifacts and taxidermy. She was also the author of several books, which she offered her patrons – most of them today would be considered "promotional materials," printed in order to promote her reading business. Lenormand spent a short time in prison for fortune telling on more than one occasion. But, somehow, this only seemed to help her notoriety. With her publications, her talent for publicity, and her head for business, Marie Lenormand would be considered an "influencer" by today's standards. She'd no doubt be a public relations wizard with social media. But, it was her talents that brought the people back again and again. Her reputation for accuracy soon brought in more patrons, and she catered to both the rich and poor, offering various price points and levels of readings. Now a celebrity seer to the French court, her personal fortune began to increase. Mademoiselle Lenormand claimed to have advised many famous persons, among them leaders of the French Revolution (Marat, Robespierre, and St-Just), Empress Josephine, and Tsar Alexander I. It is said that she told Napoleon Bonaparte that he would rise to become Emperor but would die sad and alone in exile.

She kept her rooms on the Rue de Tournon for many years, adding to the decor as her wealth grew, including several paintings she commissioned of herself by prominent artists of the time. At the age of 71, she died on June 25, 1843, leaving behind an estimated fortune of 500,000 francs (1.8 million dollars in today's buying power.) As her only surviving relative, her nephew inherited her entire estate. A devout Catholic, he burned all of her occult items, cards, and books - a true loss for historians today.

*Portrait of Marie Anne Lenormand from The Court of Napoleon by Frank Boott Goodrich, described as follows in the book: "The portrait of M'lle Lenormand ... is taken from an engraving at the Bibliothèque Impèriale, in Paris, believed to be the only authentic likeness of her in existence.*

So, did she read with or invent the 36-card Lenormand deck that we know today? No, she did not. While less is known about them, it is believed that Lenormands were based on Sybilla cards, which she may have used.

A French publisher by the name of Grimaud commissioned the French artist Grandville to create the cards known as "Sibylle des Salons" as far back as 1840.

Their inspiration was based on Austrian fortune telling and a combination of cards used there. The deck, La Vera Sibilla, is an Italian spinoff to these Austrian cards and is still popular in Italy today, second only to Tarot. The 36-card deck expanded into a 52-card deck so that playing card (very popular in Northern Italy at the time) suits and symbols could be assigned to them.

Lenormand cards weren't published as "Lenormand cards" until Mademoiselle Marie Lenormand became famous for her accurate fortune-tellings. It was after her death that they received their proper name as publishers sought to piggyback onto her reputation to make sales. In other words, it was all public relations, using a celebrity name associated with cartomancy to sell more decks of cards at a time when, legally, little could be done about it as there was no trademark protection in place.

Old advertisement for Lenormand cards, often found in novelty catalogs and in the back pages of dime-novels.

# THE CARDS

As we dive in and look at each individual Lenormand card, keep in mind the way they are read in pairs, then strung together to create a story. Lenormand cards tell a tale with simple keywords. There is no need to look at every detail of the card's imagery to find its true meaning. You simply string the keywords together to form a sentence. For example, STORK (progress/changes) + TOWER (profession/ambition/legalities) + ANCHOR (stability/settled) could mean you are making progress in your profession, leading to a more stable situation.

But before we begin creating stories with our cards, it is essential to study each one to learn their primary meaning and appreciate their down-to-earth simplicity. This simplicity is what makes reading Lenormand easier to grasp for some cartomancers.

The cards we will be examining are from my personal collection of the 1926 Carreras Fortune Telling cards. The Carreras Tobacco Company distributed these particular cards under their "Black Cat" brand of cigarettes, where a single card was included in every pack. The Carreras Fortune Telling Cards were published for W.D. & H.O. Wills, Bristol, and issued by Carreras Ltd in several sizes (narrow and wide) and in different formats (some showed the playing card associations, some the figures of people). These chromolithographic decks were printed by B. Dondorf in Germany and were based on the Dondorf Lenormand cards from the 1880s. I have both the wide and narrow versions in my collection but chose to use the narrow version for this book, which showed the playing card insert.

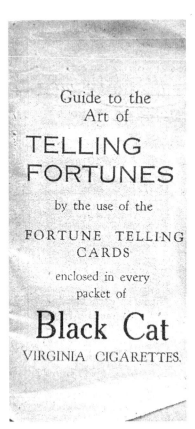

Guide to the
Art of

# TELLING
# FORTUNES

by the use of the

FORTUNE TELLING
CARDS

enclosed in every
packet of

## Black Cat

VIRGINIA CIGARETTES.

# 1 – THE RIDER

Action, movement. This card usually means that something new is "riding" into your life or that news is on its way. Change, visitors, a messenger, or that life is about to change. All the delays that you have been experiencing are about to dissipate so be prepared for whatever is about to happen or finally show up. The first card in the deck, the Rider is not usually about permanency so be prepared for him to ride back out of your life as quickly as he arrived. He brings you an opportunity that you must seize before it disappears. Be ready to act quickly. He can be a person, an event, or an action such as a sudden burst of energy or motivation.

Playing card association: 9 of hearts

# 2 – CLOVER

Luck, opportunity. Signifies good luck and fortune, most of the time showing up as a small amount of luck, as in a "stroke of luck." Hope, second chances, rewards, bonuses, or a welcome surprise. The clover stands for luck that shows up all of the sudden without warning but doesn't tend to stick around very long. When the clover appears beside another card that is on the negative side, its luck tends to rub off on the card beside it, soothing whatever the problem may be. In terms of money, the clover would represent a small amount of good fortune – something along the lines of finding a five-dollar bill in a parking lot, not winning the lottery. Can signify problems solving themselves out of nowhere. Opens the doors of opportunity.

Playing card association: 6 of diamonds

# 3 – SHIP

Movement or journey. While this card sometimes means travel, either for business or pleasure, it can also signify something sailing into (or out of) your life. Since a ship can sail both ways, it is important to look at the cards on either side of the Ship to put the meaning into context. The Ship is about pursuing dreams and goals, actively reaching out to make things happen. If you are thinking of starting a business or changing jobs, this card can mean the fruits of your labor are finally about to pay off. In other words, your ship is about to come in! Transition, change, sometimes separation, new journeys. It can literally mean an overseas trip is in the future.

Playing card association: 10 of spades

# 4 – HOUSE

Sanctuary, family. The House card is almost always associated with home and family life. Sometimes it can be your place of work or a place you think of as a safe comfort zone. If this card represents your workplace, think of it in terms of your department or what you are responsible for – not the fate of the entire company. Can also represent your community and, occasionally, your need to set boundaries within that community. The House card is your connection to all things domestic and environmental. This card often surfaces to tell you that it is time to focus on home and family in a way that is comforting to you, for your own peace of mind. The House card can also represent your own body. Security, comfort, success, neighbors.

Playing card association: King of hearts

# 5 – TREE

Health, ancestry. This is a card of well-being. It can signify physical health, mental health, even spiritual health, and wellness. However, pay close attention to the cards that fall on either side of it to determine if it is a good sign or a signal that a checkup with your doctor may be needed. Also used to mean setting down roots or a deeply rooted situation. The Tree card implies a time of growth in all areas of your life, a slow but steady growth that is both nurturing and grounding as you begin to make your way towards your goals. Strong family bonds. It may signify moving a relationship to a more permanent level – a time to welcome your chosen life partner into your family. Patience, balance, staying rooted in your beliefs and reacting to situations with maturity.

Playing card association: 7 of hearts

# 6 – CLOUDS

Confusion, contradiction. Just as we look at the skies and see a storm rolling in, the Cloud card can indicate disagreements or problems just ahead. But the clouds are also about seeing both the light and the dark of a case. The card it lands beside will determine whether you are dealing with the light or the dark side of a situation. Not a time for rushing into decisions. Since clouds can hide the truth from sight or make things appear different than they really are, it is a time of reflection and careful planning before acting. Represents things that are hidden or not made apparent. Emotionally, the Clouds card can warn of depression, fooling yourself, and self-sabotage. Confusion caused by outside influences that can cloud your judgment.

Playing card association: King of clubs

# 7 – SNAKE

Deceit, rival, wisdom. A card of deception and betrayal that is often associated with "the other woman." An enemy, the competition, or someone who is jealous of you. Most of the time, the Snake card shows up as a person, someone with dark secrets and a hidden agenda. This person is a master of manipulation, and you may not even be aware of their hypocrisy until it is too late. Distrust, sabotage, trouble, envy. However, the Snake can also be a card of wisdom. It may bring you troubles, but they have valuable life lessons attached to them. It suggests taking a diplomatic and well-thought-out approach to your problem. It is a card based on emotion rather than tangible objects. How you maneuver the situation is what keeps you from being bitten.

Playing card association: Queen of clubs

# 8 – COFFIN

Ending, division. In traditional Lenormand, this means that it is time to put an end to something. It also represents feeling stagnant, a sense of detachment, or the need to detach. It is time to let go of commitments, jobs, and people that add no joy to your life but, for whatever reason, you have been holding onto. It warns you to take a hard look at situations that just aren't going anywhere and suck up all your productivity, creativity, and motivation. Ignoring the advice of the Coffin card can lead to depression and ill-health. Negativity, bad luck, transformation, end of a relationship. In a literal sense, it can mean that something is boxed-up or encased.

Playing card association: 9 of diamonds

## 9 – BOUQUET

Gifts, recreation. Sometimes called 'Flowers' in different Lenormand decks, it is a card of happy gifts and little surprises. It represents a time of pleasure and contentment, a signal that things are going your way. The bouquet may mean small tokens of esteem offered to you, encouragement from a person singing your praises, literal bouquets at a wedding, or seeds (sometimes emotional ones) that can be planted to grow into something beautiful. The Bouquet card offers positive energy, nurturing, and blessings for new ventures. Joy, pampering, beauty, good times.

Playing card association: Queen of spades

# 10 – SCYTHE

Terminate, remove. The Scythe card literally means that it is time to "cut it out." In other words, it is a time to terminate something, whether it be an attitude or an unhealthy relationship. So, while many view this card only negatively, it can be giving sound advice about removing something that no longer serves you. With this in mind, it can be one of the most helpful cards in the Lenormand deck, providing you with guidance that you may not want to hear but is needed. Being a sharp object, the Scythe may also be a warning of an accident to come. The Scythe card can also mean something that happens suddenly or radical changes coming your way. Sudden ending, a clean break, surgery. A sharp-tongued individual. Budget cuts at work or home.

Playing card association: Jack of diamonds

# 11 – WHIP & BROOM

Argue, clear the air. Often known as the 'whip' or 'whip and broom' in traditional Lenormand decks, and is sometimes referred to as the 'rod' card. Often used to signify discord or problems in a marriage. Sweeping problems under the carpet. Whips are usually wielded more than once when used, so this card can mean repetition. For this reason, it can be a card of sex (a repetitive motion) or, for a health reading, may indicate a chronic condition – one that sticks around or keeps surfacing. In a work context, the Whip card can mean that you need to speed up your process and put an end to procrastination. It is time to confront a problem head-on and get it over with. Time to get your act together. Punishment, disciplinary actions, and blaming others.

Playing card association: Jack of clubs

## 12 – BIRDS

Communicate, visit. The Birds card is about chats, conversations, giving speeches, holding meetings - all types of verbal communication. It can also mean having a small outing or visit with a friend or short travel. Depending on the card it lands beside, it could mean a misunderstanding. The Birds encourages you to open the lines of communication and talk about things before miscommunication occurs. It can be about negotiations, problem-solving, and letting others know where you stand. On the flip side, it can also mean knowing when to keep quiet, not over-reacting to situations, and taking a cooling-off period before speaking your mind. Beware of participating in gossip without knowing both sides of the story. Talking, a date, debate, a long conversation.

Playing card association: 7 of diamonds

# 13 – CHILD

Innocent, simplistic. Used to represent a new beginning or to mark the early stages of something. This is usually when someone is just learning and has little knowledge of the subject—looking at things like a child or a student. The Child card is like the Fool card in Tarot in that it marks a time of starting on a new journey, moving in a new direction, or completely starting over. It asks you to approach the world the way a child would with spontaneity, playfulness, and a carefree attitude. Lighten up and try not to take yourself too seriously all the time. If the Child card is nestled between two negative cards in your spread, it might be warning you to plan more before starting a new project. A signal that maturity is needed. New ideas, making a fresh start, something new.

Playing card association: Jack of spades

## 14 – FOX

Caution, disguise. The card tells you to beware of something. People around you may not be as they seem. Blatant lies, deceit, and mistrust. This is the card of the trickster, the con artist, the manipulator. Be prepared, cautious, and stay aware and alert. When the Fox card appears, it tells you to investigate what lies beneath a situation – what is going on behind the scenes. A scam or fraud may be being perpetrated. On a less harmful note, the Fox can be about agility and knowing how to maneuver situations to your advantage by sitting back, monitoring your surroundings and the people involved, then acting accordingly — being clever, adaptable, thinking critically. It can mean walking into the middle of a messy situation.

Playing card association: 9 of clubs

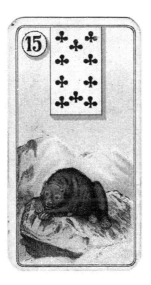

## 15 – BEAR

Protection, nurture. Think of this as the "mama bear" card - someone nurturing, protective and supportive. The Bear card is large and in charge. It represents strength, dependability, potential, and power. This can translate as a boss or someone who has power over you who asserts their authority when needed. It can extend to legal matters with the Bear standing in for a judge or lawyer. Some will look up to the Bear as a mentor, while others find her intimidating. It is also a card of abundance and protecting your finances. An authority figure, savings, cash, stocks, assets, stability, and investments. Just as bears store up and hibernate for winter, it may be telling you to work on money-saving goals and to watch your spending.

Playing card association: 10 of clubs

# 16 – STAR

Options, direction. This card is about listening to your instincts and looking at all options with clarity and a good sense of direction. The skies are clearing, and a new path is presenting itself. That thing you've been working for and wishing for is about to materialize right before your very eyes. Hope, the promise of success, contemplation, recognition, inspiration, dreams. The Star card gives you advice about thoroughly planning out your future and paying attention to the details for your wishes to come true. The Star card wants you to follow your destiny – do things that you are passionate about, both in work and play. Too much of the mundane can lead to burnout. It wants you to make a wish upon a star and then make it happen.

Playing card association: 6 of hearts

# 17 – STORK

Progress, changes. This is a card of movement and action and can often mean a change of residence. Things are changing for the better, possibly through a promotion or moving into a better position. When the Stork card appears, an upgrade is about to happen in your life. But, for change to happen, things might have to get messy for a short time. Can mean that change is needed due to feeling stagnant, and it is time for you to break away from the norm. Doesn't a stork always mean pregnancy? Not necessarily – it depends entirely upon what question was asked. It can mean a baby is coming if the Stork card falls beside the Child card. Upgrade, travel, a new addition to the household, changes for the better and learning to adapt.

Playing card association: Queen of hearts

# 18 – DOG

Friendship, faithful. Usually, this card means a friend, partner, or acquaintance. Or, depending on the reading, it could literally mean a pet. The Dog card is about trust, loyalty, relying on someone, intimacy, security, or that a new friend is on the way. However, it can also mean the way that other people view us. The Dog card can indicate that the people around you find you to be trustworthy, someone they can talk to, someone who can keep a secret. If the Dog card lands beside the Snake or the Mouse card, it might mean that someone around you is two-faced. If one word had to represent the Dog card in a Lenormand reading, it would be 'loyalty'.

Playing card association: 10 of hearts

# 19 – TOWER

Profession, ambition. In Lenormand, the Tower card has an entirely different meaning than it does in Tarot. Here, it is about rising to the top, getting ahead, having an advantage, moving up in business. Can also signify legal matters, a place of business, a corporation, an institution, or government. In fitting with these work-related symbols, it could stand for rules, red tape, and the need to go through the proper channels. Sometimes it can stand for permanency, a connection to the past, respect for tradition, and things that stand the test of time. On the emotional side, it can also mean arrogance, too much ego, and looking down on others (or being looked down upon), as well as loneliness and seclusion. It might hint at sex as the tower can be a phallic symbol.

Playing card association: 6 of spades

## 20 – GARDEN

Society, gathering. A garden is not just a place where people gather (such as in a garden party), but it is also where all your planning and hard work comes to fruition – although not without the help of others. One can plant a garden, but not much will come of it without the sun, the bees, and water. It can mean a time to appreciate the efforts of those around you. Also, a sign of a group of people: a convention, a public speaking engagement, a party. The Garden card might be offering you advice about overworking yourself – the call to get out in nature, a need for rest or a vacation either alone or with a group of loved ones. Other meanings: networking, social media, advertising, and "spreading the word."

Playing card association: 8 of spades

# 21 – MOUNTAIN

Challenge, denial. The mountain indicates that something is standing in your way. Achieving your goal will take time and won't happen without overcoming obstacles. It can mean someone who has an aloof attitude or is in denial. Might indicate that something or someone is holding you back. The Mountain card asks us to not only face up to life's challenges but to seek out creative ways to work around them. The climb may seem like a long and scary trek, but the feeling of accomplishment that comes from reaching the top of the mountain can offer a new outlook. However, the mountain doesn't always have to represent a challenge. It can foretell a large project, job, or event that, if you prepare properly for it, will be less of a hassle and easier to tackle.

Playing card association: 8 of clubs

# 22 – CROSSROADS

Choice, turning point, a fork in the road. There are many possibilities ahead of you – the only problem is that you must choose one. May signal a time of hesitation and indecision. A turning point may be just ahead, and it's up to you to weigh the pros and cons carefully. It could also suggest multi-tasking or juggling work and family. Many Lenormand readers overlook that the Crossroads card can also stand for a decision you have already made. When this happens, another choice, another crossroad lies before you – you can either continue the path of your previous decision or reevaluate, go back, and move forward on a different road. Try new things. Think outside the box. One path can throw up a roadblock on the others, so choose wisely.

Playing card association: Queen of diamonds

## 23 – MICE

Deterioration, loss. The easiest way to describe this card is to think of a mouse in your pantry stealing your food – something is being taken from you. This may indicate you are being used for money or your hospitality is being taken for granted. It can also mean that another's attitude is stunting you emotionally or spiritually. In the same way that mice slowly take over your entire house, the Mice card might suggest that a relationship shows signs of decay. It might mean a breakdown in communication or that one has begun to slack at work. Whether it is a problem in your business, home life, or attitude, deterioration is setting in, and it is up to you to nip it in the bud before it gets out of hand. Suggests: fears, theft, worries. Possibly a time to guard your health.

Playing card association: 7 of clubs

## 24 – HEART

Emotions, compassion. Love and passion are not the only meanings of this card. It can also suggest all open and loving matters of the heart: being compassionate, understanding, giving, and generous. Depending on the layout of the cards beside it, it could also be a warning not to make decisions solely with the heart. Happiness, compatibility. But despite its Valentine's Day notoriety, the Heart card isn't exclusively about love. It can represent true friendship, acts of compassion and charity for those in need, or a sense of sincere appreciation for the people in your life. It can mean acting with the best intentions for the good of others, as in the old saying, "your heart was in the right place." Putting the welfare of others above your own. Forgiveness. Reconciliation.

Playing card association: Jack of hearts

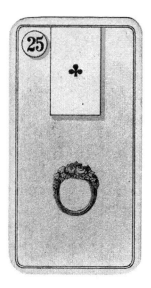

# 25 – RING

Partnership, contract. When this card turns up, thoughts immediately go to a marriage engagement. And this may be true, depending on the situation and the rest of the cards. However, the Ring card can also have a deeper meaning regarding contracts and agreements. Entering into an obligation or forming an alliance that will be long-lasting. May hint at legal agreements or paperwork that must be signed. The Ring card talks about your inner circle – the people that populate your everyday life, your community. It can sometimes mean that you need to get into a routine to avoid wasting your time just running around in circles. Think carefully and weigh your options before making commitments that you may not be able to honor. Trust, guarantee, cooperation.

Playing card association: Ace of clubs

# 26 – BOOK

Information, education. This is a card about knowledge. The knowledge may come from schooling and study, revealing a secret, or opening the mind to new ideas. Could also mean that a secret is standing in the way of true knowing and enlightenment. Signals a time of teaching, being taught, investigation, and research. From a literal standpoint (dealing with paper), it can indicate files, reports, tests, exams, accounting, and other ephemera. The Book card was originally a symbol for a book of magic, so secrecy is one of its definitions. This card can also advise you to become more open-minded, explore new ideas, and think outside the box. It can signify a thirst for knowledge both academically and spiritually. Hidden mysteries to be solved.

Playing card association: 10 of diamonds

## 27 – LETTER

Correspondence. Deals with all types of paperwork, writing, and communication. Newsletters, newspapers, articles, certificates, diplomas, and photographs. This card can mean that you are going to read something that will spark a new idea. New information will show up in the mail (or email), or payment is coming your way. Love letters, wills, Doctor's prescriptions, and mail. Might indicate a person who is a writer. The Letter card is about receiving important news soon through some formal communication. While it mainly deals with papers, phone calls fall under the Letter as well. In our modern world, the Letter can also represent blogging, social media work, and videography. It can be a reminder about keeping better records, taking notes, paying bills.

Playing card association: 7 of spades

# 28 – MAN

The male inquirer. This card represents a male asking the question of the card reader. It is often placed in the center of the nine-card spread. It can also be the love interest of the inquirer. This card can always be chosen for someone with what is stereotypically considered 'masculine traits' who is not necessarily female. Can represent someone who takes charge, is the head of the household, the head of a company or organization, or may simply stand for someone in the querent's life: a brother, father, grandfather, husband, or a male friend. Depending upon the question asked, the Man card can represent the male genitalia or health issues of a man in the querent's life. Considered a neutral card in the deck, its meaning is completely dependent on the cards around it.

Playing card association: Ace of hearts

# 29 – WOMAN

The female inquirer. The card represents a female asking the question of the card reader or someone with feminine energy. It is often placed in the center of the nine-card spread. Can be the love interest of the inquirer. It might represent a sister, mother, grandmother, wife, or a female friend. Can be a symbol for the female genitalia, women's health issues, or the health of a woman friend. Like the male card, it is considered a neutral card in the deck. Its meaning is entirely dependent on the cards around it. Some examples are: the Woman card + the Clover card would mean a lucky woman. The Woman card + the Whip card might mean a hot-headed or argumentative woman. Sometimes called the 'lady card.'

Playing card association: Ace of spades

# 30 – LILY

Peace, sensuality. The lily card is primarily about maturity, stability, and wisdom. Most of the time, it represents the older generation – those who have seen and experienced life. Relaxation, retirement, a time to slow down and enjoy life at a slower pace. It could mean a vacation. In love, the lily represents a deep and lasting love, one that is mature and stable. In terms of work and career, it indicates someone who is established in their job, possibly an expert. This card can also mean peace and approaching things decisively at a slow pace. Seeking freedom and reaching milestones in life. A time when one can harvest what they have sewn and enjoy the fruits of their labor. Some readers use the Lily card for sex and sensuality.

Playing card association: King of spades

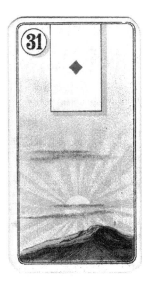

# 31 – SUN

Success, achievement. You are walking into a bright, positive future. The sun card is about achievements, being motivated, self-confidence, and being victorious over your obstacles or enemies. It can also be a sign of someone with a positive outlook entering your life – someone who brings warmth and light into the room. This person may very well be you, signaling a more uplifting time in your life filled with luck and "good vibes." Sometimes, it means it is time to shine light onto a situation and see it for what it actually is. On a spiritual level, the Sun card can mean you are seeking new paths and moving into a time of enlightenment. If you are experiencing difficult times, the Sun lets you know that your troubles are coming to an end.

Playing card association: Ace of diamonds

# 32 – MOON

Intuition, emotions. The Moon deals with things that are hidden just below the surface and are, for the most part, not visible to the public. These are often subconscious processes, hidden thoughts. Can represent psychic abilities and intuition. It also talks about other gifts that are of the mind: creativity, imagination, and dreaming – which naturally translates into the arts, as well. Emotions such as desire and falling in love may be represented. Just as the Moon affects the tides, it can influence our emotional ups and downs. The Moon card advises you to cut loose and begin exploring your fantasies and pursuing your dreams. Follow your instincts and intuition, and the Moon will guide you to what you seek, even those dreams still unknown to you.

Playing card association: 8 of hearts

# 33 – KEY

Discovery, insight. Literally, the key to something, the answer. Think in terms of passwords or ah-ha moments because this is what the key card is all about. It is discovery, revelations, and breakthroughs. You suddenly have an epiphany, and all your plans fall into place. Obstacles from the past begin to disappear. It can also be a card that highlights the card beside it – showing you the "key" to unlocking the problem before you. It could indicate that you should look for little clues and signs that will guide you in the direction you want for your life and future. The Key card brings new possibilities and opportunities – sometimes a new way of looking at things. It helps you claim your personal power and begin looking at the world through new eyes.

Playing card association: 8 of diamonds

## 34 – FISH

Commerce, freedom, sales. This is the card of money, abundance, trade, and industry. It is about success, starting your own business, or getting a promotion at work. The tide is beginning to flow in your direction and good things are coming. With abundance comes more independence and freedom. Can mean something as simple as vacationing beside a body of water. The Fish card doesn't always stand for money in the bank. It can tell that you understand the value of what you have and appreciate it. It might mean being rich in knowledge, talent, accomplishments, or possibly love and friendships. Whatever it signifies, it means that you have or will have plenty of it. It could be time to finally start that business you've been dreaming about.

Playing card association: King of diamonds

## 35 – ANCHOR

Stability, settled. The anchor means things that anchor you in life, things that nurture you and ground you. It is a card of work and getting things done. This also means dealing with everyday life, such as cleaning the house, grocery shopping, cooking, and gardening. Settling down, making a home. A touchstone that grounds you. It could possibly mean a stop, a standstill. If you plan to make a change, the Anchor card cautions you to wait a bit longer. If you are planning a trip, it suggests a postponement. On a psychological level, the Anchor card advises against becoming too rigid or close-minded in your beliefs. Let go of ideas that no longer serve you and make you a creature of the past.

Playing card association: 9 of spades

# 36 – CROSS

Sacrifice, burden. Think of having a cross to bear. Deals with life lessons and difficulties that one must overcome without the help of others. The need to give up something to achieve something greater or for the selfless good of another. Sadness, remorse, regret, and being a victim are other themes of the Cross card. It can also mean religion and faith, spirituality, and sacred things. It can signify a time in your life that you must endure some setback or difficulty – as in the phrase, "a cross to bear." Emotionally, the Cross card is about release – letting go of the things you cannot control and having faith that things will work themselves out. Can indicate a time of being tested. A time to either re-evaluate your beliefs or stand firm with them.

Playing card association: 6 of clubs

# PLAYING CARD SUITS

## HOW TO APPLY THE PLAYING CARD SUITS IN LENORMAND READINGS

Lenormand card readers differ in their opinions about applying the meanings behind the playing card Suits (Clubs, Hearts, Spades, and Diamonds). In a reading with a straightforward question, I rarely pay attention to the Suits and mainly focus on the Lenormand card itself and its meaning. In fact, in one of my early editions of my Good Mojo Lenormand Oracle, I removed the playing card Suits. However, once I realized their importance in digging out more information about what is happening behind the scenes, I added them back and found a new respect for them.

After playing cards found their way into Europe, there were regional variations of the suits, so not all cards were the same. Around the 15th century, the French developed the four Suits that we still use today. When the English adopted these four suits as "standards," there were still lingering discrepancies in the meaning behind each suit, depending on whether you were speaking to a Frenchman or Englishman. The meaning of the Hearts suit was the same. Originally called *Fleurs* in French, Clubs are still called *Fiori* in Italian (both words translate to mean 'flowers').

The Suit of Clubs represents money, career, physical activity, and obstacles that stand in your way.

Hearts are primarily related to love and relationships.

Spades include cards related to communication, travel, and legal matters.

Diamonds are related to luck, danger, decisions, risk, and reward.

## HOW THE SUITS CORRESPOND TO TAROT SUITS AND ELEMENTS

- Clubs/Pentacles/Earth
- Hearts/Cups/Water
- Spades/Swords/Air
- Diamonds/Wands/Fire

## A SHORT HISTORY OF PLAYING CARDS

To become the deck we recognize today, playing cards have undergone a drastic transformation since their first beginnings several centuries ago, mutating as they traveled from country to country.

It appears that playing cards may have had their beginning in China around the 9th AD century during the Tang Dynasty. This is also around the time when the technology of woodblock printing was invented, allowing for printed information to spread. Around 1005, sheets of paper began to replace traditional scrolls, allowing playing cards to rise in popularity. It is said that these early Chinese cards may have been influenced by oiled paper strips used for various games in Korea. Playing cards in China were usually long and narrow, and while symbols were used, they were not yet sorted into suits.

When cards reached Egypt, they added their own flair by creating abstract works of art for each card.

Jump forward to the 1300s when playing cards finally reach Europe. If you were to trace the tracks of products, you will find that the trade routes follow many of the same patterns. Products travel from China to Italy to France and then to England. Venice was one of the major trading centers during the 1300s, which is why most new finds from China would show up in Italy first who traded heavily with France. Most inventions from China usually found their way to Egypt first. However, trade routes sometimes left Egypt out of the loop. The early history of cards in Western Europe was related to the invasion of North Africa, Spain and Sicily by Islamic forces during the Mamluk Sultanate of Egypt which ended in 1517.

## A TIMELINE OF PLAYING CARDS

**1300s**: Playing cards reach Europe - in 1367, an official ordinance mentions them being banned in Bern, Switzerland.

**1377**: A Paris ordinance on gaming mentions playing cards, meaning they were so widespread that the city had to make rules to keep players in check.

**1400s**: Familiar suits start appearing on playing cards across the world—hearts, bells, leaves, acorns, swords, batons, cups, coins.

**1418**: Professional card makers in Ulm, Nuremberg, and Augsburg start using woodcuts to mass-produce decks.

**1480**: France begins producing decks with suits of spades, hearts, diamonds, and clubs. The clubs are probably a modified acorn design, while the spade is a stylized leaf.

Late **1400s**: By the end of the century, European court cards switch from current royalty to historical or classic figures.

**1790s**: Before the French revolution, the King was always the highest card in a suit; the Ace begins its journey to the top.

**1870s**: The Joker makes its first appearance as the third and highest trump in the game of Euchre.

**1885**: The first Bicycle® Brand cards are produced by Russell, Morgan, & Co. later to become The United States Playing Card Company in 1894.

## THE GYPSY WITCH FORTUNE TELLING PLAYING CARDS – A LENORMAND SPINOFF

If you are a fan of Lenormand cards, you might be surprised to find that you can easily read the cards inside that little orange and black box called The Gypsy Witches deck. It was the Chicago-based company, Frederick J. Drake & Co., that began publishing the *Mlle. Le Normand's Gypsy Witches Fortune Telling Cards back in 1894. It was a 52 card deck that was based on a 48 card interpretation of Lenormand cards by Berlin designer Danner* G. Mühlhausen, who had taken the liberty of adding 12 additional cards to the traditional 36-card Lenormand deck. So, by the time the Gypsy Witches Fortune Telling cards hit the market, the number of cards found in a standard Lenormand deck had increased, in total, by 16 cards. This was mainly done to accommodate the playing card associations and, during the redesign, most of the meanings of the cards were changed or switched around. While the cards found a home at many other publishing houses over the years, today, they are printed and distributed by USGames.

The next two pages are the cards found in a Lenormand deck and the playing card associations you'll find on each card. Many are obvious as to why they are associated with the interpretation of each because the raw energies of their meanings match up. Others aren't as "in your face" as some, but if you dig deep enough, you should find that can add layers to your reading.

## THE PLAYING CARD ASSOCIATIONS

**Cross** (6♣) = burden, suffering, sacrifice
**Mice** (7♣) = losses (health and wealth), stress, productivity
**Mountain** (8♣) = obstacle, inactivity, delay
**Fox** (9♣) = work, skills, discernment
**Bear** (10♣) = resources (including money), strength, protection
**Whip** (J♣) = sex, conflict, physical activity
**Snake** (Q♣) = betrayal, complications, disease
**Clouds** (K♣) = confusion, uncertainty, discomfort
**Ring** (A♣) = commitment, partnership, obligations
**Stars** (6♥) = inspiration, guidance, technology
**Tree** (7♥) = life, health, gradual development
**Moon** (8♥) = romance, intuition, recognition
**Rider** (9♥) = news, arrival, visitor
**Dog** (10♥) = friend, acquaintance, loyalty
**Heart** (J♥) = love, affection, generosity
**Stork** (Q♥) = improvement, relocation, pregnancy
**House** (K♥) = home, family, safety
**Man** (A♥) = male person
**Tower** (6♠) = authority, legal matters, corporation
**Letter** (7♠) = written communication, document, mail, telegram
**Garden** (8♠) = public, group, outdoors
**Anchor** (9♠) = stability, perseverance, base
**Ship** (10♠) = travel, vehicle, distance
**Child** (J♠) = young person, small size or quantity, student
**Bouquet** (Q♠) = beauty, pleasure, gift

**Lily** (K♠) = elders (especially males), maturity, serenity
**Woman** (A♠) = female person
**Clover** (6♦) = luck, chance, boost
**Birds** (7♦) = verbal communication, companionship, negotiations
**Key** (8♦) = solution, certainty, discovery
**Coffin** (9♦) = death, depression, bankruptcy
**Book** (10♦) = knowledge, secrets, research
**Scythe** (J♦) = decision, danger, separation
**Crossroads** (Q♦) = choices, diversification, junction
**Fish** (K♦) = business, transaction, independence
**Sun** (A♦) = success, vitality, self-confidence

## TEA LEAF READING SYMBOL ASSOCIATIONS

As mentioned earlier in this book, many Lenormand card meanings were derived from tasseography – coffee and tea leaf readings. In 2020, when I was working with Catherine Yronwode on our book, *The Stranger in the Cup - How to Read Your Luck and Fate in the Tea Leaves*, I noticed many of the associations were the same or, at least, similar. The symbols here are from Cicely Kent's book, *Telling Fortunes By Tea Leaves - How to Read Your Fate in a Teacup* from 1922. The only symbol that was not present was the Crossroads. For it, I've included Catherine Yronwode's definition for 'lines' from her website, The Mystic Tea Room, found at www.mystictearoom.com. *Bold indicates the Lenormand card.*

**1 - Rider**
Rider.—This brings good news from overseas of business and financial affairs.
Mounted Horseman.—A sign of good friends, luck, and advantageous offers.
**2 - Clover**
Clover.—A very lucky sign of coming good fortune.
**3 - Ship**
Ship.—News from distant lands; a successful journey; a voyage.
**4 - House**
House.—A successful transaction, a visit, a new home.
**5 - Tree**
Trees.—Good health and a pleasing assurance of coming prosperity and happiness; if surrounded by dots an inheritance of property in the country is foreshown!
**6 - Clouds**
Clouds.—These denote disappointment, failure of plans, and dismay.
**7 - Snake**
Snake.—This is an unpleasant sign of treachery, disloyalty, and hidden danger, sometimes caused by those whom you least suspect; if its head is raised, injury by the malice of a man is predicted; it is also an indication of misfortune and illness.

**8 - Coffin**

Coffin.—A bad omen of coming bereavement; a coffin with a sword beside it shows death of a soldier; with a flag, that of a sailor; with snowdrops, death of a child or infant.

**9 - Bouquet**

Bouquet.—This is a most fortunate symbol of coming happiness, love, fulfilled hope, and marriage.

**10 - Scythe**

Scythe.—This sign foreshows grief and pain.

**11 - Whip**

Whip.—To a woman this sign foretells vexation and trials in her marriage; for a man, it has much the same meaning, and severe disappointment will befall him.

**12 - Birds**

Birds.—These are significant of happiness and joyful tidings; a single bird flying means speedy news, telegrams; birds in a row on a branch or line show that there will be vexatious delay in receiving some wished-for news; birds in a circle denote cogitation followed by swift decision.

**13 - Child**

Child.—This is a sign that you will soon be making fresh plans or forming new projects; a child running means bad news or threatened danger; at play, tranquillity and pleasure.

**14 - Fox**

Fox.—This denotes that you may have an unsuspected enemy, possibly disloyal dependents; sometimes it means theft and trickery.

**15 - Bear**

Bear.—A journey north, sometimes prolonged travel.

**16 - Stars**

Star.—A lucky sign; if surrounded by dots, wealth and honour are foretold.

**17 - Stork**

Stork.—In summer, this bird tells you to beware of robbery or fraud; in winter, prepare for bad weather and a great misfortune; a stork flying predicts that whilst you hesitate in coming to a decision, a profitable chance is lost, the news of which will speedily reach you.

**18 - Dog**

Dog.—This symbol has many meanings which must be read in accordance with the other symbols; in a general way this sign indicates adverse conditions, the thwarting of life's chances, unfortunate love affairs, family misfortune and money troubles; a large dog sometimes signifies protection and good friends; a small dog, vexation and impatience.

**19 - Tower**
Tower.—This predicts an advantageous opportunity through which you may rise to a good position in life.
**20 - Garden**
Garland.—A sign of happiness, love and honour.
**21 - Mountain**
Mountain.—This gives promise of the realisation of a great ambition and of the influence of powerful friends; many mountains indicate obstructions and sometimes powerful enemies in your career.
**22 - Crossroads**
Lines.—If straight, progress; if wavy, uncertain path.
Cross.—You must expect to meet with hindrances and obstacles in the way of your desires.
**23 - Mice**
Mice.—These indicate danger of poverty through fraud or theft.
**24 - Heart**
Heart.—A sign of coming happiness through the affections bringing joy into your life, or satisfaction through money, according to other signs near.
**25 - Ring**
Ring.—With dots around, a contract or a business transaction; with the figures of a man and woman, an engagement or wedding is foretold.
**26 - Book**
Book.—An open book shows a desire for information and a mind ever on the alert to understand new theories and facts; a closed book is a sign of expectancy.
**27- Letter**
Letters.—These are shown by oblong or square tea-leaves, initials near give the name of the writer; with dots around they will contain money.
**28 - Man**
Man.—You may expect a visitor.
**29 - Woman**
Women.—With bad signs, several women mean scandal; otherwise, society.
**30 - Lily**
Water Lily.—This flower proclaims a declaration of love.
Arum Lily.—This flower stands for dignity, expectancy, and calm.
Belladonna Lily.—This flower is a sign of hope, love, happiness, and the leading of an upright and honorable life.
**31 - Sun**
Sun.—This promises happiness, health, success in love, prosperity, and the beneficial discovery of secrets.

### 32 - Moon

Moon.—A crescent moon denotes good news, fortune, and romance; for a man it predicts public recognition and honor.

### 33 - Key

Key.—Circumstances will improve, things will become easy, and your path will be made smooth; you may hope for success in whatever you have on hand; a key at some distance from the consultant denotes the need for the assistance of good and influential friends in times of difficulty.

### 34 - Fish

Fish.—News from abroad; with other signs of movement, emigration; a starfish is a sign of good luck.

### 35 - Anchor

Anchor.—A pleasing symbol of good and loyal friends, constancy in love, and the realization of your wishes; an emblem of safety to a sailor.

### 36 - Cross

Cross.—You must expect to meet with hindrances and obstacles in the way of your desires; sorrow and misfortune are also indicated by this symbol.

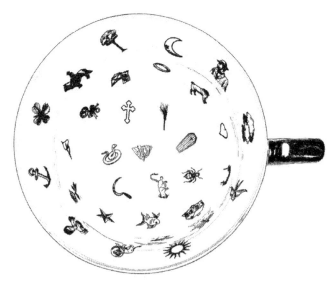

A modern Fortune Telling Teacup with Lenormand symbols inside by Australian artist Karin Dalton-Smith. www.teawithkarin.com

# HOW TO READ THE CARDS

While there are many systems of reading Lenormand cards, the one train of thought that is agreed upon is that they should not be read like the Tarot. Tarot cards have many-layered meanings in each card, little stories told in each card position. Also, Lenormands have no reversed meanings. So, if you pull a card and it is upside-down, feel free to turn it around so that it is upright.

The Lenormand cards are more simplistic in their approach. Each card may be a word in a sentence. Sometimes, a simple phrase. The cards are read from left to right, starting with the beginning of the tale on the left and concluding on the right, unless a specific spread directs you to read it differently.

Lenormands are read in pairs. Because of their simple meanings, when paired together, the meanings become more profound and more complicated. For example, HOUSE + MICE. House by itself usually just means a home. But when you put the MICE card into the equation, it becomes evident that something is going on inside the house that may make it less of a sanctuary. This might literally mean that the house is infested with pests. It could also mean a moocher is living inside that is disrupting finances and family life.

Now, swap out the MICE card with the ANCHOR, and a completely different scenario unfolds. HOUSE + ANCHOR signals a happy, stable, and secure home life. The anchor shows that those in the house are settled down.

In other words, one card acts as a noun – the other, an adjective and gives more description (like all good adjectives do) about the noun card. HOUSE + STORK (movement, change residence) sounds like a move is just around the corner, and the house may go up for sale soon. Now, let us add another card to that. Imagine the querent asking, "Will my house sell quickly at the asking price?" The three cards that come up are HOUSE + STORK + CROSS (a sacrifice). This may hint that for the house to sell quickly; the price may need to drop. Or that if the sellers want their asking price, they may have to give up the idea of selling quickly.

The most important thing to remember is to read the cards from left to right, look at their primary meaning, and string together the story they are telling you. All stories have a beginning, a middle, and an end - and so will your card spreads.

## THE THREE CARD SPREAD

The three-card spread is a simple reading that will answer just one question. Many Lenormand card readers use the three-card spread to answer "yes" and "no" questions. Three cards of a positive nature mean "yes." Three cards of a more troublesome nature mean, "No." Two positives and one negative would indicate a maybe, which leans towards "yes." Two negatives and one positive card imply that more than likely, the answer is "no," but there is the possibility of turning things around.

The other way to read the three-card spread is the same example already given about the querent wanting to sell their house with HOUSE + STORK + CROSS. It tells the outcome of a particular question.

Another example might read like this: A woman wants to know if her boyfriend will propose marriage. The three cards that are drawn are LOVERS + BOUQUET + RING. You don't need to know Lenormand cards to see that those three words strung together mean that, yes, he is going to propose. The LOVERS shows the couple in question, The BOUQUET is a gift, and the RING is a symbol of partnership or contract (or a proposal.) Sometimes, the RING can signify the beginning of a business partnership or contracts that need to be signed. However, considering the question that was asked and the two cards that fell in front of it, it most definitely addresses a future marriage proposal.

Another sample of how to do a 3-card reading deals with reading a chain of events with the cards falling as TOPIC + CAUSE + EFFECT. Meaning, the first card tells you what the reading is about; it is the TOPIC. The second card is what CAUSED this situation to happen, and the third card would be the EFFECT - in other words, what happened next because of the second card. Another way to look at these three cards is THE SUBJECT + THEN THIS HAPPENED + WHICH MADE THIS HAPPEN.

## THE FIVE CARD SPREAD

The five-card spread is another simple layout. While it doesn't give in-depth insight like longer spreads, it conveys a little more information than the three-card spread. In the five-card configuration, the center card is your focus card. The two cards to the left of the center card show what transpired in the past or what influenced this current situation. The two cards to the right of the center explain what happens next or what the best course of action might be.

## THE CROSS SPREAD

The cross spread also uses five cards but in a completely different way. The card placed in the center of the reader is the significator card, which we will preselect. Choose THE MAN for a male querent or THE WOMAN for a female querent and place the card in the center of your surface. If reading for a gay client, some readers will pull the opposite sex card to signify the querent, leaving room for the same-sex card to appear somewhere else in the spread.

Card 1 will be placed above the querent, card 2 falls to the left, card 3 is on the right, and card 4 is beneath.

Some readers decide not to preselect the center card and allow a random card from the deck to take its place. Sometimes it can contribute to the story. Whichever method you decide to use is ultimately a matter of preference. If you do decide to choose a random card for the center, place that card first before you proceed with 1, 2, 3, and 4.

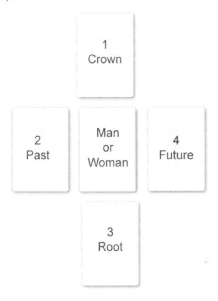

1. What is "hanging over" the seekers head. This may be something out of their control or that they are unaware of. Could also be a constant source of concern or worry.
2. The Past – what led up to the current state of events.
3. The root of the problem. This is a "what lies beneath" card and signifies the real cause of the situation.
4. The Future – what lies ahead

## THE NINE CARD SPREAD

The nine-card spread is probably one of the most popular spreads in Lenormand, other than the Grand Tableau. The center card, number 5, is often purposely placed. For example, if the querent is a man, use the man card in the center. If a woman, use the woman card. Others might choose a card that deals with a situation. If the reading is about love, place the heart card in position 5. Have a question about a job? Place the tower card in the center. Of course, you also have the option of letting the center card fall organically.

There are a few ways to read the cards that surround the center card. If you want to read the cards showing the past and the future, then you will have two pairs of cards falling before the center card: 1,2,3,4. Remember, Lenormands are often read in pairs, so 1+2 go together, and 3+4 go together, telling a story about the past. 6+7 gives hints for the future, while 8+9 shows the probable outcome of the situation.

You will notice that inside the nine-card spread, the cross spread also makes an appearance.

Others choose to read the nine-card spread in this way: 1+2+3 (1 is a noun, 2 an adjective, 3 another adjective)

4+5+6 (4 describes the querent in the 5 position and 6 describes them further.) In other words, 4 is an adjective, 5 a noun (the subject), and 6 and adjective.

The pattern continues with:
7+8+9 (7 is a noun, 8 an adjective, 9 another adjective.)

A third example of reading a nine-card spread is by reading the cards from top to bottom.

1+4+7 is the past

2+5+8 is the present

3+6+9 is the future

The biggest trick is to discover which layout works the best for you. Once you find it, you will more than likely use that layout most of the time but can turn to the other examples when you are looking for additional information.

Im Literatur- & Kunst-Comptoir in Berlin sind folgende, höchst interessante Schriften erschienen und können durch alle Buchhandlungen bezogen werden:

## Karten der berühmten Wahrsagerin

### Mlle. Lenormand aus Paris,

mit denen diese berühmteste Wahrsagerin ihres Jahrhunderts die wichtigsten Ereignisse der Zukunft vorhergesagt.

36 feine lithographirte Karten, nebst einer leichtfaßlichen Erklärung, wodurch es Jedem möglich ist, sich selbst die Karten zu legen und so seine Zukunft kennen zu lernen, in elegant ausgestattetem Etui.

Preis 10 Sgr.

Mit diesen Karten verkündete Mlle. Lenormand Napoleon seine Größe, sowie vielen Fürsten und Großen ihren Untergang.

1840 wurde von Mlle. Lenormand als das Todesjahr Friedrich Wilhelm III., verstorbenen Königs von Preußen bezeichnet.

Diese Karten, nebst Anleitung und Erklärung bilden den ersten Theil der Wahrsagekunst der Lenormand und werden den Besitzern des zweiten Theils (die Physiognomik und Chiromantie) als unentbehrlich empfohlen; doch werden die resp. Käufer gebeten, darauf zu achten, daß sie die in obiger Handlung erschienenen Karten erhalten, da nur diese allein die richtigen sind.

An old German advertisement for Lenormand cards.

## THE GRAND TABLEAU

In French, Grand Tableau means "the big picture." This layout uses every card in the deck and shows the overall picture of the querent's life. It answers questions on many topics and covers the past, present, and future. The spread shown in our illustration is the Grand Tableau, known as the 9x4 spread. To verbally deliver a Grand Tableau reading may take up to 1 ½ to 2 hours.

First, choose whether you want to use a fate line. What is a Fate Line? A fate line is usually read outside of the reading and about things in your life that you cannot change or are out of your control. While these cards may still pertain to the Grand Tableau reading, the 36th card is almost always the "ending" in a reading. Meaning, the fate line doesn't finish the bigger picture story – it simply gives you extra messages about the things you cannot change. Choosing to use a fate line is personal taste. Fate lines are found in other Lenormand spreads as well. When you decide to lay out the cards in four rows of eight cards (an 8x4), you will end up with four extra cards as your fate line. This example works in a standard, 36-card deck of Lenormand.

Variations on the Fate Line. Some readers use this last line to signify a different message and do not use it as a fate you cannot change. It can also be interpreted as a life lesson that needs to be learned, a special message to pay attention to, or a general "theme" line describing a person's life pattern. Some say it tells what direction your life is heading.

There are several examples of how to read the Grand Tableau. We are going to cover two of them. The main thing to remember is that you are deciphering a giant puzzle. The key to success is to uncover when one topic about the querent's life ends, and another begins.

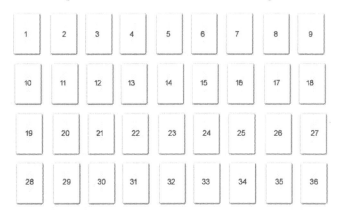

## EXAMPLE 1

This is a vertical past and future reading. The center line – 5,14,23,32 is the present. All the cards that fall to the left of this center line are the past. All the cards that land to the right of the center line is the future. While it is visually a vertical reading, you will still read from left to right. For example, when reading the past, you go in this order: 1,2,3,4,10,11,12,13,19, etc.

## EXAMPLE 2

This is a querent landing reading. Notice that we don't say this is a "placement" reading like described in the nine-card spread. The man or woman card is allowed to fall organically in the spread. Let's say you are reading for a woman. The woman card might not appear until, for example, the 23rd card. This means you have a lot of information about the past and less about the future. If the querent falls very low in the layout (such as the 35th card), it can sometimes mean they are not meant to know the future at this time.

This particular spread is entirely read from left to right. No consideration of the vertical rows or a center line is used as it is in example 1. Simply start with the first card and continue reading until you reach the last card. If you choose to use one, the Fate Line is still read as "extra info."

## LENORMAND HOUSES

When you spread out the cards in the Grand Tableau, you are laying each card within, what is called, a Lenormand House. For example, the first card you put down is in the house of The Rider (the first card in a Lenormand deck.) The second card is placed on the house of The Clover (the second card in the deck) and so on and so on. Imagine it as having two decks of Lenormand cards. The first deck, you have glued face-up and in order onto a poster board in a Grand Tableau pattern. This would be your 'house board' you would use to lay your second deck of cards onto. What this does is immediately pair one Lenormand card with another since they are traditionally read in pairs. If the Bouquet card lands on the first house of The Rider, someone is about to show up with a gift. The Snake card on the house of The Rider? Someone deceitful approaches. If the Fish card lands on the second house of The Clover, it might be a good time to buy a lottery ticket. And this continues throughout the entire layout of 36 cards, giving you detailed information with every card pulled. If you have a hard time remembering their order, Grand Tableau cloths with this house pattern are available online and in many metaphysical stores.

## THE FOUR CORNERS

The cards that fall in the four corners of the reading are sometimes used to show the overall theme of a person's life. A quick glance at these four cards can give you a brief, overall message about what the inner cards may speak of. Experienced Lenormand readers can quickly assess the four corners and know the outcome of a reading and some of the events that led up to it. In other words, the four cards create a summary.

## THE NEAR AND FAR

The near and far method deals with how close certain cards are to the signifier card - the signifier cards being the Man card or the Woman card. If the Fox card, for example, is four or more cards away from the Woman (if a woman is receiving the reading), then she is safe for now. But, if the Fox card is beside her or just a few cards away, treachery approaches, and it is time for her to start looking over her back. If you are also using the past and future method and the Fox card is behind her, there's nothing to worry about because the event has already happened. However, the cards in front of her might explain if she knew about this past deceit and how it affects her in the present, if at all.

There are many other ways to read the Grand Tableau and different layouts for the Lenormand cards. Feel free to branch out and find more in-depth instructions. There are many books, internet articles, websites, and YouTube videos explaining the cards and the various ways to read them.

# A LIBRARY OF LENORMAND

Now that we've covered all the basics – the history of Lenormand, the meaning of each card, and how to read the cards in multiple layouts, I wanted to offer you a glimpse into the many different Lenormand cards published throughout the years. While there are several modern decks you can buy today, including my own *Good Mojo Lenormand Oracle*, I've selected a few of the older, rarer decks that you might not usually see. If you ever happen upon these decks for sale, expect to pay hundreds if not thousands of dollars. I have managed to acquire a few older decks in my collection at a fair price, but there are hundreds of types of Lenormands that were printed and sold since the 1800's – many you will only find in a museum.

Printed in Germany by the defunct publisher, "Ensslin & Laiblin, Reutlingen." – their name appears on card 36. The numbering is not the usual Lenormand numbering, and a few cards are non-standard. Printed around 1880. In total there are 39 cards including additional man & woman cards as well as the cards' meanings.

The Ship and The Rider cards from the 1880's Ensslin deck.

The Snake card from an Ensslin 1899 deck

The German company Wuest was a large publisher of playing cards in the 19th century up until the 1920's. The Lenormand Fortune Telling Cards by Wuest are unique. While some report that the first Weust deck was in 1885, earlier versions of their deck can be found going back to 1860.

Published by Vereinigte Stralsunder Spielkartenfabriken, Stralsund, c.1890. The imagery used in this deck of cards is identical to an earlier Dutch manufactured deck.

Gypsy Sabina Self-Explaining Fortune-Telling Cards, 1904,
by The American Illustrating Co.

A German deck from the 1850's, later reprinted in America in the 1920's.
In 2003, the cards were revised and released by Bernd A. Mertz.

Dondorf's "Wahrsage-Karten" Madame Lenormand fortune-telling cards
with verses. c.1911-1933. The back design has the letters 'B.D.' for
Bernhard Dondorf company.

Le Petit Cartomancien manufactured by B.P. Grimaud, Paris. 1890

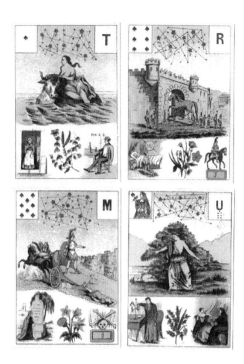

The Grand Jeu de Mlle Le Normand has been published by B.P. Grimaud
since c.1860. First published in France around 1845.

Old Gypsy Fortune Telling Cards, Whitman Publishing Co., 1940

Madame Morrow's Fortune Telling Cards, 1886, McLoughlin Bros.

Old Gypsy Fortune Telling Cards by Whitman Publishing, 1940.

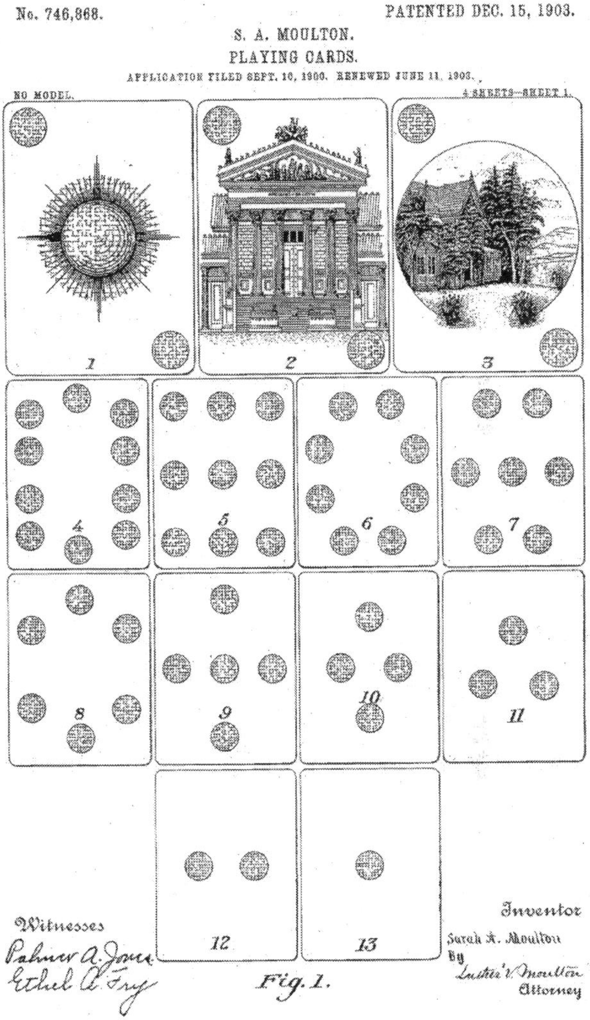
No. 746,868.
PATENTED DEC. 15, 1903.
S. A. MOULTON.
PLAYING CARDS.
APPLICATION FILED SEPT. 10, 1900. RENEWED JUNE 11, 1903.
NO MODEL.
4 SHEETS—SHEET 1.
1
2
3
4
5
6
7
8
9
10
11
12
13
Witnesses
Palmer A. Jones
Ethel A. Fry
Fig. 1.
Inventor
Sarah A. Moulton
By
Luther V. Moulton
Attorney

Cartomancy playing cards invented and patented by Sarah A. Moulton and Luther V. Moulton, of Grand Rapids, Michigan, 1903. *"The object of my invention is to provide playing cards with a single series of symbols adapted to serve in place of the symbols of the ordinary cards and at the same time well adapted for educational purposes and for cartomancy."*

Title of deck is unknown. Printed in Paris by Ch. Didot around 1890 and
contains German verses and astrological symbols.

Schmid Lenormand. Printed in a limited edition in Germany but never
went into reprint. Rare. 1950

# CONCLUSION

When I started writing *Lenormand Basics*, the plan was to create a pocket guide with basic information on the cards. But, as I began the process of working on the illustrations for the project, I was reminded of my genuine love for the Lenormand cards. So, out of my own curiosity, I continued researching the topics I wanted to cover. It led me to decks I had never seen, a larger understanding of the card meanings, and, of course, a few trips to eBay to expand my collection of vintage Lenormands.

All my book projects begin with research – even for material that I am already familiar. Because, no matter what the topic - you will always find new knowledge, some bits of information you'd forgotten, or data you wholly misunderstood. Each time I write a book, it leaves me knowing more about the subject than when I began. So, I become both the teacher and the student during the process. I know that writing this book has made me a better Lenormand card reader. I hope that reading it did the same for you.

# BIBLIOGRAPHY

**George, Rana.** *The Essential Lenormand: Your Guide to Precise &
Practical Fortunetelling.* Llewellyn Publications. 2014

**Greer, Mary K.** "A New Lenormand Deck Discovery." *Mary K.
Greer's Tarot Blog.* July 12, 2013

**Katz, Marcus** and **Goodwin, Tali.** *Learning Lenormand.* Llewellyn
Publications. 2013

**Kent, Cicely.** *Telling Fortunes By Tea Leaves - How to Read Your Fate
in a Teacup.* Dodd Mead and Company. 1922.

**Matthews, Caitlin.** *The Complete Lenormand Oracle Handbook:
Reading the Language and Symbols of the Cards.* Destiny Books.
2014

**White, Gregory Lee.** *The Good Mojo Lenormand Oracle Companion
Book.* White Willow Press. 2013.

**Yronwode, Catherine.** *"A Basic List of Tea Leaf Symbols."* The
Mystic Tea Room. www.mystictearoom.com

*Fortune Telling with Cards, Dice and Dominoes.* Wehman Bros. 1920.

*Remarkable Women of Different Nations and Ages.* John P. Jewett &
Company. 1858

# OTHER RESOURCES

*The World of Playing Cards.* https://www.wopc.co.uk

*The Lenormand Museum.* http://lenormand-museum.com. No longer
online.

*The Game of Hope.* Reproductions of Lenormand cards.
http://gameofhopelenormand.bigcartel.com/

**Dalton-Smith, Karin.** Lenormand teacups.
https://www.teawithkarin.com/

Made in the USA
Monee, IL
01 August 2023

40240576R00050